The Mind of a Poet

Earl D. Simpson

For Brendell Ellison, Jayla Simpson, and Gabrielle Herford

To all the readers of my first book "Poetry from the Heart:"

It was your request that encouraged me to write this book. For you, I included a special section titled "Ask Earl"

Table of Contents

Again

I thought the first time
Perhaps would be enough
But my love for the spoken word
It was like a rush
I gain much support
Made some new friends
From my point of view
The situation was a win
I hope everyone who reads
Find what you're looking for
Maybe, for a brief moment
My words will be your cure
It took a little time
For that, I do repent
I'm back once again
Giving you one hundred percent

The Beggar

He stood on the corner
Holding an empty can
Begging for spare change
From his fellow man
I moved closer
To get a better view
The beggar appears healthy as me
As healthy as you
Why wouldn't he be ashamed?
Were there no options left?
He begged from a small kid
Who couldn't support himself
Could I pass by this human?
Still considering myself meek
Well, the Holy book says,
"If a man doesn't work, he shouldn't eat.

Change of Season

Watching the birds as they fly south
A change of season is coming soon
Insects go beneath the ground and hide
Another season is on the rise
The weather changes as the temperature falls
Animals give each other mating calls
All being symbolic of nature
New life forms during incubation
Everything is in precise order
One season comes, the other being the departure

Chaos

4

Please help us all
A society without laws
From one generation to the next
Where it's generic to be barbaric
No punishment for a crime
No loss of life or serving of time
The world is in an array
Only the strongest can stay
The weak leaves like the wind
Where your worst enemy is your closest friend

Deep in Love

5

Remembering our quality time
Lately, I've been thinking
It's like being in quicksand
You've got me sinking
Deeper and deeper in love
Until I don't know what to do
My mind is tangled and twisted
I'm always thinking of you
One glance in my direction
That was all it took
Just like fishing
You have me hooked
The center of my attention
Top of the line
No doubt about it
I've found a perfect dime

Excuses

One excuse after another
Until you didn't even bother
Excuses, excuses, excuses
Some I could never imagine
As they rolled off your tongue
They came in perfect fashion
You thought of every reason possible
For why you didn't do what you said
Some I never heard before
The only exception was being dead
Thinking of many excuses
Some too incredible to say
Using an unlimited supply
Multiple excuses for each day
Do yourself a great favor
Coming from you, I don't believe a word
Treat your excuses like bird seeds
Feed them to the birds

First

First, that's your place
I couldn't do anything
If it wasn't for your grace
Time, talent, and treasure
My whole life too
I don't own anything
It all belongs to you
A debt I can't repay
The greatest loan
Letting me borrow a life
To call my own
That's why you're first
In everything I do
Acknowledging your kindness
If only for a moment or two

The Gate

We formed a single line
Now, we must wait
There are millions of people before us
Trying to enter the gate
An enormous variety of ethnics
Both young and old
The gate is open to everyone
Because we all have souls
Calling one name after another
As the line inches on
The sound of footsteps
Seems to be playing a soft song
It's been a long journey
Sometimes life can be tough
When it's our turn at the gate
I hope we have done enough

He Stepped In

When I couldn't find a friend
He stepped in
When life seemed hopeless
I sought the end
He stepped in
Blessed Savior, King of Kings, Prince of Peace
Stood on my side
My life in His hands to guide
Oh! Merciful One
To sacrifice your own Son
It was by your grace
All problems, I can face
Into my heart, you entered
Saving the soul of a sinner.

Hint

10

Be pleased to believe
Thrill to give
Grow in what you sow
Trust is a must
A lifetime lease on peace
Blessed to be a guest

If it Happens to You

As we already know
No two people think alike
What I think is wrong
You may think is right
It was a horrible experience
An unexpected surprise
Just like a gamble
Losing with one roll of the dice
It left me in pain
A long lasting hurt
I'm not giving up
My whole net worth
If it happens to you,
Is there someone to talk to?
Handle it yourself
That advice is easy to say
When situations are going the right way.

Inside, Outside

Whether you're inside looking out
Or outside looking in
Circumstances are not as clear
As they should have been
When it's all lovely
Everything is in place
But what's really happening
Is moving at a luring pace
Thoughts can be deceptive
Giving the wrong impressions
Making you wish for the worst
Your mind, having no detection
Being greedy and making bad decisions
Caused you to lose all you had
There's no one else to blame
Leaving only yourself to be mad
Your bright future is gone
Now, there is nothing left
You were concentrating on others
When you should have been concentrating on yourself.

The Interview

In the lobby, I waited
For my name to be called
I couldn't help to notice
The certifications on the wall
Finally, my name is called
I am to be interviewed next
Hopefully, my mind is sharp today
I need to be at my best
I walked into the next room
I'm asked to sit in a chair
I have to stay focused
Have to be aware
Into the room, the interviewer walked
She's professionally dressed
I hope I have the right answers
Otherwise, this interview will be a mess
First question asked
I gave a speedy reply
Oops! Wrong answer, I thought to myself
I said that/and didn't know why
I hesitated at the next question asked
Knowing I can't wait too long
Because the reply I give
Will most definitely be wrong
Questions being asked in an original fashion
I'm starting to feel at ease
I had a nervous start
Now, this interview is a breeze
The interview is over
She stood and shook my hand
"Welcome to the team," she said,
"I can always use a good man."

In the Past

14

What's in the past
Has already been done
Best forget about it
Continue to have fun
You can't reverse the outcome
You can't turn back time
Why make yourself miserable,
When it's so easy to decline?
What's in the past
Has happened and gone
Forcing the issues
You may find yourself all alone
Filled with sorrow, sad as can be
Wondering where your happiness went
Well, you were living in the past
When you should have been enjoying the present.

Love (the antidote)

15

Stored in your heart
Is the antidote for hate
Impatient to be released
As if it can't wait
The greatest power on earth
Love can conquer all
Only takes a small dose
For your adversaries to fall
With an indefinite supply
Love was made to give
So open your heart
Love is not to be sealed

The Magician

16

The magician stood before me
My view was very clear
Pulled a rabbit from his hat
Puff! Made the rabbit disappear
I must see that again
It had to be some kind of trick
All I saw was smoke in the air
And a ball of fire that flicked
That goes to show
Things aren't always what they seem
Your eyes may deceive you
If you know what I mean

Many

We are many
We are plenty
Having different faces
Living in strange places
Disguised in various shapes and forms
Our intent is not to harm
Many we are
The near and the far

The Message

18

The message is a blessing
Know it to sow it
Keep it to reap it
Give it to live it
Share it to spare it
As truly as it will occur
For I am only the messenger

More than Friends

I have this feeling for you
That I need to express
When I tried to tell you
My words were a mess
I wanted to explain
Hoping you would comprehend
I wanted a serious relationship
Not just you being my friend
How can I get my point across?
I offer all that I have
My gesture of love for you
Although, you consider me just a pal
It's a prolonged experience
Meanwhile, I can only wait
Hoping our friendship will turn into love
I will keep my faith

No Comparison

When comparing yourself to others
You're only asking for trouble
Why even bother
To complicate a situation further?
You're one of a kind
That's your peace of mind
Be happy with yourself
Never compare you to anyone else

Nowhere

I came to a dead-end
Went into reverse
That's exactly where I had been
I turned to my left
It took me nowhere
I was all by myself
Surrounded by nothing but air
I turned to my right
It was dark, dark as night
A pitch black scene
With nothing in sight
Where am I?
I stood still with no place to go
Somehow I was put here
How can this be so?
I must move on
Thinking I had enough
I couldn't turn left or right
I ascended straight up

Obstacles

22

Obstacles are barriers placed in the way
They can be removed by grace
Can't prevent but will delay
Coming with higher prices to pay
Counted one by one
Probably, is a long list
In the back of our minds
That's where most obstacles exist

One Wonderful Day

It is a wonderful day
Better than yesterday
It is one wonderful day
Listen to what I have to say
I woke up this morning
The sun was shiny and bright
Thought of my obligations
I knew everything would be alright
This day is so fine
It changed my state of mind
What a blessing this day will become
Turned my whole day into fun

The Party

24

Clouds of smoke filled the air
Evidence of a party was everywhere
People were dancing to a groove
Swirling as their bodies moved
They talked but I couldn't hear a sound
The music was so loud there voices were drowned
The DJ spent one record and on to the next
The crowd was pleased as he honored their requests
It's a joyful time, I must admit
If I stay, my future is a bottomless pit
I stepped backwards without a cheer
It's best for me to leave from here

The Platform

My temperature was really warm
As I nervously stood on the platform
I'm in the spotlight
I'm all uptight
It's my turn to perform
I'm on the platform
I calm down and performed a great show
From the first second, it was all systems go
Everyone stood in amazement
Just as I predicted
All my fears had diminished
They all applauded when I finished
I left the crowd begging for more
As I politely exit the door

Relaxed

At the end of the day, I sat on a recliner,
My arms resting by my side.
I tilt my upper body backward as my feet elevate.
Thoughts of the day travel through my mind,
As the radio plays.
I can hear but I'm not listening.
The music only comforts me.
Thoughts enter and exit my mind quickly.
What did I accomplish today?
Could I have done more?
Questions go on and on.
Some I don't have an answer for: Why? I don't know.
My eyelids get heavier, I feel myself drifting away.
For a while, I won't have a worry at all.
I'll be totally asleep.
In my mind, I'll visit places I have never seen.
I won't have to question myself until I wake up again.

Room 114

I drove for many miles
I'm ready to rest
I passed a few hotels
Deciding to stop at Hotel Best
I walked in the hotel lobby
The clerk asked if I wanted a single or double
"Whatever," was my reply,
"Neither would be any trouble."
She greeted me warmly
While appreciating my patience
Meanwhile, I filled out a registration form
That required my identification
"Room 114," she said
As she passed me the key
She also gave me a remote control
Knowing I wanted to watch TV
When I saw that king size bed
I made a gigantic leap
As soon as my head hit the pillow
I was fast asleep
I probably didn't move an inch all night
Because I woke feeling refreshed
What a long, peaceful night
I see why this place is Hotel Best
Well, it's checkout time
I need to be on my way
I'll never forget room 114
The room that saved my day.

The Same

We are one of a kind
With the same aspects
You don't have to believe me
Read your own text
We all are human
From hence we came
Although we hide our feelings
We show emotions without shame
Each having our own mind
Yet, we are one of a kind
On the same page
As we all age

Smile

Put a smile on your face
Be exceedingly glad
Why live with a frowned face
Causing problems from being mad?
Smiling doesn't take much effort
Less than it takes to eat
Difference being, you can still smile
Even if you don't have teeth

So Proud

You're the reason why
I hold my head so high
You make me so proud
I'm walking in the clouds
You're part of me and I'm part of you
My world consists of only two
I could go on and on
Never leaving you alone
I have an idea that's quite clever
Remain with me forever

Still

I stood still as life passed me by
I didn't try to move
I stood still and this is my reason why
I had nothing to prove
Still as I am
Not determining my own fate
What's in my future
Still, that's how I wait

Suppose

32

Suppose you lost everything you had
Would that make you sad?
Living in the world the way you entered it
With nothing, only a world of sin
All your possessions gone in one swipe
Disappeared like a thief in the night
Could you pretend to be in a poker game and fold?
If so, what becomes of your soul?
Just suppose!

Survive

You said that you believed in me
As though you really had a care
Everything that you did
Was for your own welfare
As long as I did it your way
It all was fine
I watched your back
Even though you didn't watch mine
It was a chess game
I always let you win
The outcome was already determined
Before the game began
If you survive or not
You're on your very own
I'm no longer beside you
You're all alone

Touched

34

A feeling came over me
One that I couldn't explain
Not knowing what it was
Only that it was not humane
My heart beat rapidly
As tears filled my eyes
I felt like crying
Without a reason why
I shook and trembled
Never been this afraid
Lord! Help me
I'm in a frantic stage
I heard a voice from above
Expressing His abundant love
"Don't worry my son," He said,
"For you have work to do.
"Bring others to Me
"The many and the few."
As my final option
I fell to my knees
My body and mind united
My soul was pleased

Trophy

If a man's status
Is measured by the trophies he has won
Although, they were given to him
In a contest merely for fun
How did he compare to others
Could that describe him best?
If that being the result
His greatest trophy beats in his chest

The Truck Driver

I follow an endless yellow line
Delivering much needed freight
Leaving one particular area
Crossing into another state
Covering forty-eight out of fifty
It couldn't be finer
With the exception of Alaska and Hawaii
Enters my big, red Freightliner
I blew at a fellow truck driver
He's driving a Mack
He gave me a quick nod
And blew his horn back
I've been driving for hours
A truck stop is in sight
I pulled my truck over
To rest for the night
My dock appointment is tomorrow
I got plenty of time to spare
Where will my next drop be?
It has to be somewhere

Twenty Years Ago

Twenty years have passed since you went away
I was a youth then, now my hair is gray
Twenty years since I last saw your face
The way you left was a shameful disgrace
Now, you've returned to be all mine
If only you would be so kind
Twenty years is a long time to wait
Although we did meet by faith
You left without saying bye
Not even an explanation as to why
Asking to enter my life again
To be anything besides a friend
As sure as you reap what you sow
My answer is no.

Two Rounds of Tae Kwon Do

I entered the ring
Stood in my corner
Looking across the opposite side
There stood my opponent
I'm a little nervous
My jitsu is wet
It's not from water
It's from sweat
Hopefully, the bout goes my way
That is my will
Only have two-three minute rounds
To display my combat skills
The bell sounded
We met in the middle of the ring
The referee watched closely
As my opponent took a swing
I felt the wind from his punch
Knowing I'm at risk
I moved backward a few inches
Just enough to make him miss
The rest of the round went back and forth
As we exchanged mighty blows
Who will win this contest?
Nobody in the crowd knows
First round over
Really, I'm glad
Only way to defeat this warrior
Is for me to get mad
The bell sound again
We started round two

Fight still up for grabs
Who will win? No one knew
He came out show boating
Tried a fancy trick
I moved just in time
To connect with a side kick
I felt a sense of relief
I was very pleased
As my opponent staggered around
Before he dropped to his knees
The referee sent me to my corner
As he started to count to ten
I wanted this match very much
I got the win

Unconcerned

40

No thoughts, no worries
Conscience clear as the air
Whatever the circumstances
You don't care
All for yourself
No feelings at all
No, not one
You are the unconcerned

The View

41

Your eyes are wide open
Yet, you look through a veil
It's transparent, yet made of many layers
It's motionless, yet it swirls
It's your view of this world

The Visitor

42

As I lay partially awake
My bed began to shake
It was dark and I couldn't see
Someone else was in the room with me
Who are you?
What do you want?
Do you have a reason for being here?
Or do you just want to haunt?
There was a certain calmness
That I could almost see
It was beyond this world
It was heavenly
What a peaceful feeling
When he came near
As suddenly as he came
He would also disappear

The Vows

You both stood before the minister
You both accepted the vows
Knowing you weren't ready
And wouldn't be for a while
Yet you said, "I do,"
To the questions that you were asked
Now, changing your mind
Wanting to take your reply back
By morale, you're obligated
By law, you're bound
That person standing next to you
Is the mate you have found
This is your blessed day
As the world revolves around you
Because on this day
You have become two

We Crossed Paths

44

Every encounter with another human
As odd as it may seem
Left a lasting impression
If you recognize the lesson
This is no coincident
This union was meant
Whether long or brief
It's your benefits to keep
You learn from everybody else
That makes you look closer at yourself
Think of the aftermath
Now, you know why we crossed paths

Word of Mouth

We settled the deal
Agreed on the terms
Word of mouth and a hand shake
The agreement was confirmed
No pen and paper
It was a verbal agreement
That was just fine
I didn't have the slightest idea
That you wouldn't keep your word
Tried to reverse the whole situation
When I knew what I heard
I kept my composure
Didn't even get mad
I got the worse deal possible
Yes, I was had
I learned a valuable lesson
This knowledge, I most certainly lacked
No matter who I do business with
Be sure to sign a contract

Ask Earl

I am taking advantage of this opportunity to communicate with my readers. Often, I am asked questions concerning my poetry. So, I've taken this opportunity to compose my responses to the most frequently asked questions.

1. Why do I write poetry?
I consider my writing as a gift from God. This is my way of thanking Him and sharing my talent with everyone.

2. When did I first discover an interest in poetry?
I was 10 years old and in the fifth grade. My reading class had to recite poems that were written by famous poets. I felt an immediate connection.

3. What are my favorite topics to write about?
I don't limit myself to certain topics. I write about what I feel, hear and see.

4. How long does it take me to write a poem?
I can write a poem very quickly; however, I usually make some changes.

5. What's next?
I will consider writing lyrics and ghostwriting.